Whoosh!

Author:

Ian Graham studied applied physics at City University in London. He then received a postgraduate degree in journalism, specializing in science and technology. Since becoming a freelance author and journalist, he has written more than one hundred children's nonfiction books.

Artist:

David Antram was born in Brighton, England, in 1958. He studied at Eastbourne College of Art and then worked in advertising for 15 years before becoming a full-time artist. He has illustrated many children's nonfiction books.

Series creator:

David Salariya was born in Dundee, Scotland. He has illustrated a wide range of books and has created and designed many new series for publishers in the UK and overseas. David established The Salariya Book Company in 1989. He lives in Brighton with his wife, illustrator Shirley Willis, and their son, Jonathan.

Editor: Jamie Pitman

Editorial Assistant: Mark Williams

© The Salariya Book Company Ltd MMX

No part of this publication may be reproduced in whole or in part, or stored in a retrieval system, or transmitted in any form or by any means, electronic, mechanical, photocopying, recording, or otherwise, without written permission of the publisher. For information regarding permission, write to the copyright holder.

Published in Great Britain in 2010 by
The Salariya Book Company Ltd
25 Marlborough Place, Brighton BN1 1UB

ISBN-13: 978-0-531-20505-1 (lib. bdg.)   978-0-531-13785-7 (pbk.)
ISBN-10: 0-531-20505-3 (lib. bdg.)   0-531-13785-6 (pbk.)

All rights reserved.
Published in 2010 in the United States
by Franklin Watts
An imprint of Scholastic Inc.
Published simultaneously in Canada.

A CIP catalog record for this book is available
from the Library of Congress.

Printed and bound in Singapore.
Printed on paper from sustainable sources.
1 2 3 4 5 6 7 8 9 10 R 19 18 17 16 15 14 13 12 11 10

SCHOLASTIC, FRANKLIN WATTS, and associated logos are trademarks and/or registered trademarks of Scholastic Inc.

PAPER FROM
SUSTAINABLE
FORESTS

You Wouldn't Want to Climb Mount Everest!

Written by
Ian Graham

Illustrated by
David Antram

Created and designed by
David Salariya

A Deadly Journey to the Top of the World

Franklin Watts®
An Imprint of Scholastic Inc.
NEW YORK • TORONTO • LONDON • AUCKLAND • SYDNEY
MEXICO CITY • NEW DELHI • HONG KONG
DANBURY, CONNECTICUT

Contents

Introduction   5

Mount Everest   6

Into the Death Zone   8

Picking the Team   10

Testing Times   12

Nepal   14

Base Camp   16

Moving Supplies   18

The Plan for the Top   20

The Mallory Mystery   22

The First Attempt   24

The Backup Plan   26

On Top of the World   28

Glossary   30

Index   32

Introduction

The year is 1952, and you are a skilled climber from Great Britain. When you're not at work, you head for the mountains. You have climbed many peaks in the Alps, a rugged mountain range in central Europe. But you dream of traveling to the Himalayas in Asia to climb Mount Everest, the highest mountain in the world. Every attempt to reach the top of Everest has failed, but there is a team of Swiss climbers on the mountain right now. You have heard a rumor that if the Swiss fail to reach the summit, a British team will be the next to try. You've spent many years training for just this opportunity. But will you be chosen to join the British team? It would be impossible to climb Everest by yourself, so you can't go unless you are invited!

I'm moving up in the world!

Klumpf!

Mt. Everest

China

India

MOUNT EVEREST is in the Himalayas, a vast mountain range that stretches across six countries in Asia.

5

Mount Everest

With a peak that's 29,035 feet (8,850 meters) above sea level, Everest is the world's highest mountain. The British named it after Sir George Everest, who had led the Great Trigonometric Survey of India from 1830 to 1843. As a surveyor, Everest's job was to measure the landscape of India so that accurate maps could be made.

In Nepal, the mountain is called Sagarmatha, which means "Goddess of the Sky." The Tibetans call it Qomolangma, which means "Mother of the Universe." In 1856, it was declared the world's highest mountain, and the race was on to climb it.

Summit

South Summit
A dome of rock just below Mt. Everest's summit

Everest

Sir George Everest

George Everest (1790–1866) spent more than 25 years surveying India. It is not known whether he ever saw the great mountain that was named after him.

FLAG CLOUD. A white triangular cloud called the "flag cloud" appears on the east side of Mount Everest in winter and spring. Its shape tells climbers how fast the wind is blowing at the summit.

South Col
A gap between Everest and Lhotse

Lhotse
The fourth-highest mountain in the world

Nuptse

Lhotse Face
The western face of Lhotse, a wall of glacial ice

Western Cwm
A valley carved out by a glacier

Khumbu Icefall
Part of the Khumbu glacier

Theodolite

Handy Hint
Check your ropes and knots—your life may depend on them.

THEODOLITES. These instruments were used to measure angles for the Great Trigonometric Survey. A theodolite weighed more than half a ton, and it took 12 men to carry one.

Into the Death Zone

If you begin to climb Mount Everest, you risk being buried by snowfalls or falling into hidden crevasses—deep cracks in the ice. Higher up the mountain, more dangers await you. There's less oxygen at higher altitudes—the air is so thin that just walking a few steps makes you gasp for breath. At the summit, it can be so cold that bare skin freezes in seconds! The region above 24,000 feet (7,300 m) is so dangerous that climbers call it the "Death Zone." You can only survive at this altitude for two or three days.

IF YOU HEAR a rumbling sound, run! It could be an avalanche—a mass of snow sliding down the mountainside.

Rumble!

Rumble!

Shiver!

THE AVERAGE TEMPERATURE at the top of Mount Everest is -33 degrees Fahrenheit (-36°C), but it can fall as low as -76°F (-60°C).

How long am I going to have to hang around here?

Hold on a minute!

Slip!

Whoosh!

CRAMPONS. Above about 16,000 feet (5,000 m) in the Himalayas, ice and snow cover the ground all year round. Climbers wear sets of spikes called crampons on their boots. The spikes stick into the ice. Don't forget to put them on, or you'll slip and fall!

AVOID CLIMBING Mount Everest between June and September and between November and March. The weather is at its worst during these times. You would face heavy snowstorms, thick clouds, hurricane-strength winds, and avalanches.

Picking the Team

If the Swiss attempt to climb Everest fails, the British will give it a try in 1953. Their expedition would be led by John Hunt, a British army officer. Hunt's first job is to choose his team of experienced male climbers between the ages of 25 and 40. You are delighted when you receive a letter inviting you to be one of the team's ten climbers. A doctor, a physiologist, and a cameraman will travel to Everest with you. All 13 men are from Great Britain or other Commonwealth countries. (The Commonwealth is a group of countries that were once part of the British Empire.) Later, one more person will be invited to join the team, bringing the total to 14.

THE JOINT HIMALAYAN COMMITTEE organizes British attempts to climb Mount Everest. It selects John Hunt to head the 1953 expedition because he is a good all-around mountaineer and an experienced military leader.

EDMUND HILLARY is a bee-keeper from New Zealand. An experienced climber, he took part in an Everest expedition in 1951.

TOM STOBART will make a film of the expedition, because there is already a lot of public interest.

MICHAEL WARD is the expedition's doctor. He is also a good climber, so he will join the climbing team if anyone drops out.

Testing Times

n December 1952, you go to Switzerland with John Hunt and two other climbers to test clothing and equipment. You take eight types of boots and try a different pair each day. The four of you swap clothes and discuss what works best. You test tents by trying to put them up in a blizzard. The day before you come home, you hear that the Swiss team has failed to reach the summit of Everest. The British expedition is on!

GLOVES. The climbers will wear three-part gloves. The inner layer is a loose-fitting silk glove, which is covered by the second layer, a woolen mitten. A windproof cotton gauntlet forms the outer layer.

BOOTS. Two types of boots are made for the expedition. One is a light boot for the first part of the climb. The other has extra insulation for colder conditions.

What's the verdict, then?

THE AIR NEAR THE TOP of Everest is very thin, so your team will use bottled oxygen to help you breathe more easily. You try it out after your trip to Switzerland. You wear a set of oxygen tanks on your back and breathe through a pilot's face mask.

Lightweight metal tanks

Economizer helps conserve oxygen

Valves control pressure and air flow

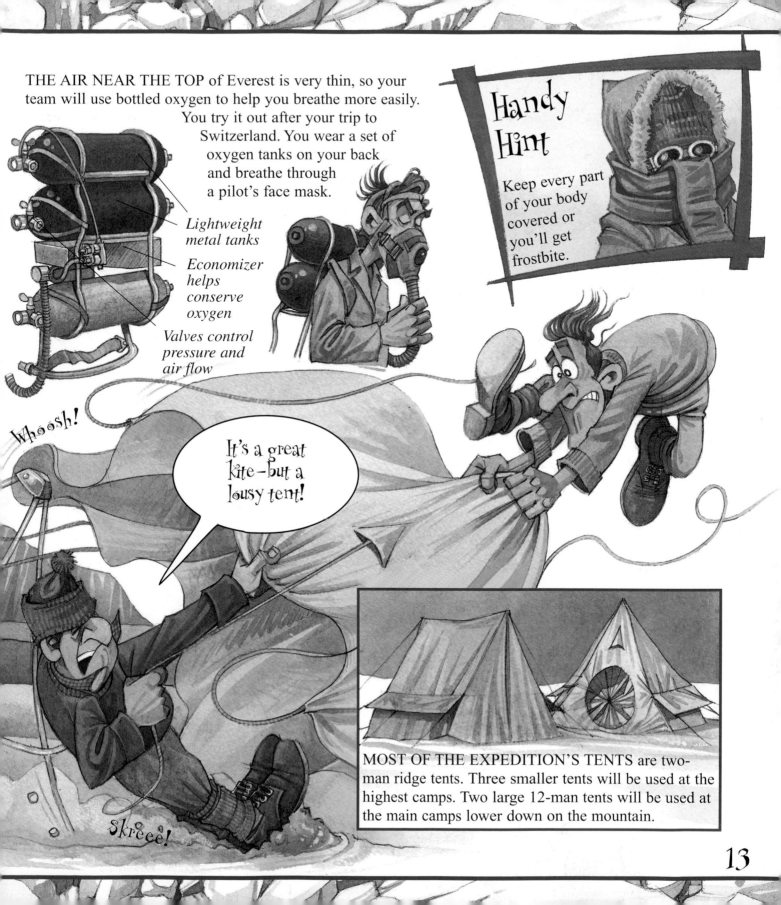

Handy Hint

Keep every part of your body covered or you'll get frostbite.

Whoosh!

It's a great kite—but a lousy tent!

Skreee!

MOST OF THE EXPEDITION'S TENTS are two-man ridge tents. Three smaller tents will be used at the highest camps. Two large 12-man tents will be used at the main camps lower down on the mountain.

Nepal

The climbers travel to Kathmandu, Nepal, by sea and then by air, along with 7.6 tons of supplies packed into 473 cases. The supplies will have to be carried on foot from Kathmandu to Mount Everest by 350 porters and 36 Sherpas. The walk will take 16 days. Sherpas are a people from the foothills of Mount Everest. They are very skilled climbers.

The Sherpas will carry the supplies to camps higher up the mountain. Their leader, or *sirdar*, for this expedition is Tenzing Norgay. He is 38 years old and this will be the sixth time he has been to Everest. He has worked on almost every Everest expedition since 1935. He nearly reached the summit with the unsuccessful Swiss expedition.

Handy Hint

Don't wear brand-new boots—you'll get blisters.

WHEN THE SHERPAS arrive, they line up for inspection wearing a variety of clothes collected from earlier expeditions. They wear ski hats and masks, berets, and brightly colored sweaters.

TENZING NORGAY is asked to become the 14th member of the climbing party because of his experience and climbing ability. He has more experience on Everest than any other Sherpa and has climbed to within 1,000 feet (305 m) of the great mountain's summit.

THE SUPPLIES are divided up between the porters and Sherpas. The packs are weighed to make sure they are not too heavy to carry. The average load is 60 pounds (27 kilograms) per person.

15

Base Camp

On March 10, 1953, the expedition begins its march from Kathmandu to the foothills of Mount Everest. Every morning, you start walking at 6:00. The kitchen staff races ahead to find a place to prepare the next meal.

When you reach the foothills of Everest, your team sets up a base camp near a Buddhist monastery. You and the other climbers will train here for three weeks so you can get used to the altitude.

TRADITIONAL HEAD STRAPS are used by the porters to carry large loads.

Deep breath ...

Pant!

WHEN YOUR TEAM ARRIVES, local people line up to be treated by your doctor, Michael Ward. He pulls rotten teeth and treats lots of minor illnesses.

GRIFFITH PUGH, the physiologist, puts you through a "maximum work test." He times you while you run uphill until you feel like your lungs are bursting.

Handy Hint

Don't let your beard grow or your oxygen mask won't seal itself against your face.

Who are you calling "Abominable"??

THE PORTERS are paid for their hard work. The same day, they begin the long walk back to their villages across Nepal.

THE MONKS are full of stories about the Yeti, or Abominable Snowman, a mysterious ape-like creature that they believe lives in these mountains.

Moving Supplies

Sherpas and your team members constantly trek up and down the mountain as you move supplies to camps higher up. Each time, you have to cross one of the most dangerous obstacles on the mountain— the Khumbu Icefall. The icefall is a constantly moving river of huge blocks of ice. The blocks of ice are separated by deep crevasses, and they groan and crack as they move. Every morning, the icefall has moved so much that a new route has to be found to cross it. One day you can easily step across a crevasse. The next day, you'll have to build a bridge to get over it.

THE ICEFALL is so difficult and dangerous to cross that bridges and ladders are used in some places. They have to be strong enough to hold the weight of a climber and the load he carries on his back.

After this, I deserve a lunch break!

> Let's hope the icefall doesn't live up to its name!

Handy Hint

Use your ice axe to test the ground in front of you. Deadly crevasses can be hidden by a thin layer of snow.

CRAMPONS are essential for climbing on ice. The metal spikes stick into the ice and keep the boots from slipping.

SUNLIGHT reflected by snow and ice is so bright that you have to wear dark glasses called snow goggles. Some of the Sherpas have made their own snow goggles from cardboard and cellophane.

The Plan for the Top

On May 7, the expedition leader, John Hunt, summons his team to the dining tent. He presents his plan for the climb to Everest's summit. The first attempt will be made by Tom Bourdillon and Charles Evans. The two men will climb to the South Summit—a dome of rock that's 335 feet (100 m) below the top of the mountain. There, they'll decide whether it's safe to push on to the summit. If they turn back, Tenzing Norgay and Edmund Hillary will make the second attempt. After the briefing, everyone settles back into their daily routine.

The Daily Routine

DAYTIME ACTIVITIES are planned around meals. It's so cold that you stay in your sleeping bag when you're not eating or training.

MOISTURE from your breath freezes to the inside of your tent at night. Sometimes you are woken by ice falling on you as the morning sun warms the tent.

A SHERPA brings you a mug of steaming hot tea first thing in the morning.

BREAKFAST is ready at 8:45—a bowl of porridge followed by bacon and eggs or fried cold cuts.

Wakey wakey!

Slurp!

So this is it!

Handy Hint

Don't forget to wear your goggles or you'll get snow blindness.

LUNCH is at noon. You have soup, salami, and cheese, washed down with coffee.

Munch!

IT'S TIME FOR TEA at 4:00 p.m. You have tea, cookies, and maybe some fruitcake.

SUPPER is served at sundown. You eat soup and canned steak and kidney pie, followed by coffee and fruitcake.

BETWEEN MEALS, you write letters home. It's so cold that the ink in your pen freezes.

The Mallory Mystery

As the climbers prepare for the final assault on Mount Everest's summit, they wonder whether they will find signs that other climbers have beaten them to the top. In 1924, George Mallory and Andrew Irvine climbed to a height of 28,000 feet (8,500 m). Then a snowstorm struck and they were never seen again. No one knows whether they reached the summit before they died. Between 1921 and 1953, about 175 climbers and Sherpas have died on the mountain. Many of their bodies are still there, because it's too dangerous to carry them down.

AT BASE CAMP, Mallory's team was photographed in street clothes. But when Mallory and Irvine attempted to climb to Everest's summit, they wore many layers of silk, cotton, and wool to protect them against the cold.

Handy Hint

When you're outside, don't touch metal with your bare skin or you will stick to it!

MALLORY was one of the most experienced climbers of his time. He took part in all three British expeditions to Mount Everest in the 1920s.

IRVINE was very good at repairing things, especially oxygen equipment.

IN 1999, MALLORY'S BODY was found on a rocky slope at a height of about 26,800 feet (8,170 meters). The items found with his body included his snow goggles, a tin of lozenges, and a watch. His camera and notebook were lost, so whether he reached the summit is a mystery.

The First Attempt

n May 26, Tom Bourdillon and Charles Evans set out from Camp 8, at a height of 26,000 feet (7,925 m). Later that day, they become the first climbers ever to reach the South Summit.

Tired and running low on oxygen, they realize that there isn't enough daylight for them to reach the summit and then return to Camp 8 before nightfall. They desperately want to reach the summit, but they know that it could cost them their lives. They turn back. On the way down, Evans slips. He hurtles down the slope, sweeping Bourdillon off his feet. Incredibly, Bourdillon manages to jab his ice axe into the snow and save them both.

Tumble!

Fssssshhhh!

Handy Hint

Make sure you keep yourself tightly roped to another climber.

SETTING UP A CAMP near the top of Mount Everest quickly drains a climber's strength. A task that would take a few minutes at sea level takes over an hour in the thin, freezing air.

Woosh!

WHEN EVANS AND BOURDILLON return to Camp 8, they are totally exhausted. They have to rest for some time before they begin to recover.

AS YOU MOVE supplies up the mountain, you discover an abandoned Swiss camp. You look for useful equipment and find cans of sardines (above). Tasty!

THE TEAM LEADER at the Advanced Base Camp uses a radio to keep in touch with climbers higher up the mountain (right).

The Backup Plan

HILLARY AND TENZING pause to catch their breath before moving supplies up to Camp 9.

AT CAMP 9, they make coffee and eat canned apricots. They have to thaw the frozen apricots on their stove.

OXYGEN. They have so little oxygen left that they can allow themselves only four hours' supply for sleeping.

Tenzing and Hillary have already been moving up the mountain from the Advanced Base Camp, just in case the first attempt on the summit fails. Now it's their turn. They each carry a set of oxygen tanks and a 40-pound (18-kg) pack of supplies. The air is so thin that it's a huge effort just to walk while carrying such a heavy load. They set up Camp 9 at 27,900 feet (8,500 m). After a meal, they settle down for the night. The temperature is 17 degrees below zero (-27°C). The freezing wind batters their tent and makes it almost impossible to sleep. After a restless night, they are tired and cold, but cheered by the thought that they are now within striking distance of the summit.

BACK AT THE ADVANCED BASE CAMP, you look up at the mountain and wonder whether Hillary and Tenzing have survived the night.

On Top of the World

At 6:30 a.m. on May 29, 1953, Tenzing and Hillary crawl out of their tent. They cross the last ridge and come to a steep cliff that will become known as the Hillary Step. Hillary wedges himself into a crack in the rock and works his way up to the top. After he helps up Tenzing, the two men make the final climb to the summit. Although Hillary is a step ahead, they agree to say that they reached the summit together. Tenzing buries some chocolate and cookies in the snow as an offering to the gods, and Hillary leaves a cross. Hillary takes three photographs and they begin the long journey down.

HILLARY'S BOOTS freeze solid the night before the final climb. He heats them on the stove to thaw them out before he puts them on. Tenzing keeps his boots warm by wearing them all night.

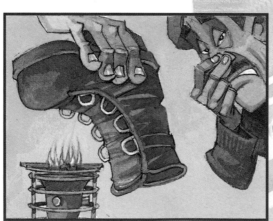

Flag of the United Nations

Flag of Great Britain

Flag of Nepal

Flag of India

Handy Hint

Don't forget to take a camera with you to prove how high you were able to climb.

YOU ARE THRILLED when Hillary and Tenzing return safely with news of their success. There are handshakes and hugs all round.

It's not the mountain we conquer, but ourselves.

THE CLIMBERS arrive at London Airport on July 3. Climbing Everest has made Tenzing and Hillary famous all over the world.

EDMUND HILLARY AND JOHN HUNT were awarded knighthoods by the newly crowned Queen Elizabeth II. Tenzing Norgay received the George Medal. In 1954, Tenzing became the first director of field training at the Himalayan Mountaineering Institute in Darjeeling, India. In 1961, Hillary set up a charity for the Sherpa people. Tenzing died in 1986. Hillary died in 2008.

Glossary

Advanced Base Camp A camp on Everest at the base of the Lhotse Face.

Altitude Height above sea level.

Avalanche A big mass of snow that breaks loose and slides down a mountain.

Blizzard A heavy snowstorm with strong winds.

Buddhist A person who follows the teachings of the spiritual leader known as the Buddha (the Enlightened One), who lived in India around 550 BC.

Cellophane A thin, transparent sheet made from plants.

Col A mountain pass between two peaks or a gap in a mountain ridge.

Commonwealth An organization of countries, most of which were once part of the British Empire.

Crampons Metal spikes fitted onto boots to give a climber a better grip on ice.

Crevasse A deep crack in a glacier.

Cwm A valley that was carved out of a mountain by a glacier.

Death Zone The part of a mountain above 24,000 feet (7,300 m), where there is too little oxygen in the air to support human life for more than a few days.

Expedition A journey organized to achieve a particular goal.

Frostbite Damage to flesh caused by extreme cold.

Gauntlet A protective outer glove.

George Medal An award for great courage that's given to civilians from Great Britain or the Commonwealth.

Glacier A huge sheet of ice that moves slowly over land.

Himalayas A mountain range that includes many of the highest mountains in the world. The Himalayas extend into six countries, including India, Nepal, and China.

Icefall A jumble of frozen blocks of ice. Icefalls are created when a glacier moves down a steep slope.

Insulation Material used to keep heat from escaping.

Knighthood An honor given by the British monarch to a man as an award for a great achievement. Knights are given the title "Sir."

Maximum work test A test to see how much a person can exercise before becoming exhausted.

Physiologist A scientist who studies how living organisms work.

Porter A person employed to carry baggage.

Ridge tent A tent with a pole that extends across the middle of the roof, forming a ridge.

Sherpa A member of a group of people living in Nepal and Tibet, famous for their mountaineering skill.

Snow blindness A painful eye condition caused by looking at bright sunlight reflected by snow and ice.

Snow goggles Dark glasses worn to prevent snow blindness.

Summit The highest point on a mountain.

Survey To make very accurate measurements of an area.

Theodolite An instrument used by surveyors for measuring angles very accurately.

Yeti The Abominable Snowman, a legendary ape-like creature that some people believe lives in the Himalayas.

Index

A
Abominable Snowman 17
Advanced Base Camp 25, 26
avalanche 8, 9

B
base camp 16, 17, 22
boots 12, 15, 19, 28
Bourdillon, Tom 20, 24, 25
Buddhists 16

C
cameraman 10
clothes 12, 15, 22
Commonwealth 10
crampons 9, 19
crevasse 8, 18, 19

D
Death Zone 8, 9
doctor 10, 16

E
Evans, Charles 20, 24, 25
Everest, Sir George 6

F
flag cloud 6
food 16, 20, 21, 25, 26
frostbite 13

G
gloves 12

H
Hillary, Sir Edmund 10, 20,
  26–29
Hillary Step 28
Himalayan Mountaineering
  Institute 29
Himalayas 5, 9
Hunt, John 10, 12, 20, 29

I
ice axe 19, 24
Irvine, Andrew 22, 23

J
Joint Himalayan Committee 10

K
Kathmandu 14, 16
Khumbu glacier 7, 18
Khumbu Icefall 7, 18, 19

M
Mallory, George 22, 23
maximum work test 16
meals 20, 21

N
Nepal 6, 14, 17

O
oxygen equipment 13, 17, 23, 24,
  26

P
payment 17
physiologist 10, 16
porters 14, 15, 16, 17
Pugh, Griffith 16

Q
Qomolangma 6

R
radio 25

S
Sagarmatha 6
Sherpas 14, 15, 18, 19, 20, 22, 29
snow goggles 19, 21, 23
South Summit 6, 20, 24
Stobart, Tom 10

T
tents 12, 13, 20, 26, 27, 28
Tenzing Norgay 15, 20, 26–29
theodolite 7
Tibet 6

W
Ward, Michael 10, 16

Y
Yeti 17